Tax Policy and Investment

Tax Policy and Investment

Kevin A. Hassett

The AEI Press

Publisher for the American Enterprise Institute

WASHINGTON, D.C.

1999

ISBN 9780-84477-086-4

THE AEI PRESS
Publisher for the American Enterprise Institute
1150 Seventeenth Street, N.W., Washington, D.C. 20036

Contents

FOREWORD, *R. Glenn Hubbard*   vii

ACKNOWLEDGMENTS   ix

1 INTRODUCTION   1

2 BACKGROUND   3
    A Brief Primer of Neoclassical Theory   3
    Early Empirical Results   5
    The Challenge and the First Wave
      of Responses   8
    Lessons from the Time-Series Data   11

3 NEW IDENTIFICATION STRATEGIES   17
    Using Cross-Sectional Variation to
      Identify Tax Effects   18
    Measurement Error in Fundamental
      Variables   19
    Misspecification of Adjustment Costs   24
    Heterogeneity of Capital Stock   30
    Summing Up   31

4 ARGUMENTS FOR AND AGAINST LOWERING TAXES
ON CAPITAL   33
Tax Reform Today Could Remove
Distortion   33
Investment Incentives Are Bad because of
Interasset Distortions   34
Failure of Investment Incentives because of
Liquidity Constraints   35
Price Elasticity of Capital Goods   40
Bondholders   41
Too Much Capital   43

5 POLICY IMPLICATIONS   47
Low Inflation as an Investment Subsidy   47
Moving to a Consumption Tax   49
Temporary Tax Incentives?   50

6 CONCLUSIONS   53

NOTES   55

REFERENCES   59

ABOUT THE AUTHOR   71

Foreword

Economists, policymakers, and business executives are keenly interested in fundamental tax reform. High marginal tax rates, complex tax provisions, disincentives for saving and investment, and solvency problems in the Social Security program provide reasons to contemplate how reforms of the tax code and other public policies toward saving and investment might increase economic efficiency, simplify the tax code, and enhance fairness. Many economists believe that gains to the economy from an overhaul of the income tax or from a move to a broad-based consumption tax can be measured in the trillions of dollars. Most conventional economic models indicate a potential for large gains from tax reform.

While many economists agree broadly on the simple analytics of tax reform, they are in much less agreement on such key empirical questions as how much saving or investment would rise in response to a switch to a consumption tax, how much capital accumulation would increase under a partial privatization of Social Security, how reform would affect the distribution of taxes, and how international capital markets influence the effects of tax reforms in the United States. This lack of professional consensus has made the policy debate fuzzy and confusing.

With these concerns in mind, Diana Furchtgott-Roth and I organized a tax reform seminar series at the American Enterprise Institute beginning in January 1996. At each seminar, an economist presented new empirical research on topics relating to fundamental tax reform. These topics include transition problems in moving to a consumption tax, the effect of taxation on household saving, distributional effects of consumption taxes in the long and short run, issues in the taxation of financial services, privatizing Social Security as a fundamental tax reform, international issues in consumption taxation, distributional consequences of reductions in the capital-gains tax, effects of tax reform on pension saving and nonpension saving, effects of tax reform on labor supply, consequences of tax reform on business investment, and likely prototypes for fundamental tax reform.

The goal of the pamphlet series in fundamental tax reform is to distribute research to a broad audience. Each study in the series reflects many insightful comments by seminar participants—economists, attorneys, accountants, and journalists in the tax policy community.

I would like to thank the American Enterprise Institute for providing financial support for the seminar and pamphlet series.

R. GLENN HUBBARD
Columbia University

Acknowledgments

I thank Glenn Hubbard and Diana Furchtgott-Roth for helpful comments and Fred Smith for making this work possible. Alex Brill provided yeoman research assistance, and Elizabeth Cooper, secretarial support. Portions of this study are drawn with permission from Hassett and Hubbard 1997 and from Cohen, Hassett, and Hubbard 1998.

1
Introduction

Proponents of fundamental tax reform in the United States have long believed that the current income tax discourages economic growth and that alternative systems could raise equal revenue with fewer distortions. While trying to convince lawmakers of this view, these advocates have faced a significant problem: until recently, scant irrefutable scientific evidence documented the damage done by the current system or the positive benefits of previous reforms for efficiency. Each responsible academic claiming evidence that tax policy reforms can improve the economy has been offset by a responsible academic maintaining that a reform will have little or no effect. This back and forth has soured public perception of the credibility of tax reformers. The case against reform is often fairly persuasive at first glance, and supporters of tax reform can easily be made to look like snake-oil salesmen.

The laws of economics (and physics) suggest that the economy can grow faster only if the quantity or quality of the key inputs to production—capital and labor—grows faster. To demonstrate that a tax reform will have a positive effect on economic growth, one must show clear, positive links between the reform and the likely behavior of investors and workers. Unless the reformer can show that workers will work harder, firms will hire more workers and purchase more capital, and workers and capital will become more productive, the case for reform has not been made. Among these possible links, the one between taxation and the investment behavior of firms has been the front line of the battle over U.S. tax policy for the past decade, probably because of two factors. First, business investment is economically important. It is a powerful stimulus to wages, productivity, and economic growth; extreme declines in investment have coincided with every major postwar recession. Second, government policy could have a tremendous effect on business investment. The labor supply, that other key determinant of economic growth, is immutably tied to population growth in the long run, and most economists view large changes in population growth or dramatic improvements in labor quality as unlikely, given the kinds of tax reforms that have been debated. Productivity, the final channel, was assumed to be exogenous by pioneering growth theorist Robert Solow; while this view may no longer be the consensus among macroeconomists, an empirically verified alternative view has yet to emerge.

Against this backdrop, investment tax credits (ITCs), special investment "reserve" funds, and accelerated depreciation allowances have been the rule rather than the exception in most developed countries since World War II. Yet, until recently, economists have struggled to find a significant impact of tax policy on investment.

Now the consensus finds that tax changes can have a significant positive stimulative effect on investment demand. Several independent and complementary studies have collectively identified and remedied serious problems in previous work, problems that led researchers to false conclusions. This monograph chronicles how the conventional wisdom has been changed and outlines the implications of our new understanding for future tax policy.

2
Background

Although the empirical economic literature on investment has a long history, the modern debate begins with the work of Aftalian (1909), Clark (1917), and Fisher (1930). Providing support for the early accelerationist school, Aftalian and Clark observed that business investment is highly correlated with changes in business output; Fisher's neoclassical theory highlighted the importance of the trade-off that firms make at the margin between the cost of raising more money and the benefit of the profit generated by an extra machine. The debate between these two schools provides a useful introduction to the literature relating tax policy to investment. Even recently, many observers (for example, Clark 1993) have argued the likelihood that tax policy does not significantly affect investment and that the differing points of view inevitably echo the accelerationist debate.

A Brief Primer of Neoclassical Theory

The simplest neoclassical argument is really a lesson in elementary economics. According to the theory, a firm weighs the costs and benefits of purchasing a machine today and holding it for one period. The firm invests when the benefits exceed the costs.

3

A simple example can demonstrate the economic logic underlying the concept of user cost. Let the firm operate for one year, after which it will sell any acquired capital and will close itself down. The firm will buy new capital at the beginning of period t at price q_t and sell it at the beginning of the next period at a different price, q_{t+1}. While the firm uses that capital, the machine depreciates from wear and tear. Again for simplicity, depreciation of capital takes place at the beginning of the period; the firm spends δq_t to replace the worn-out δ units of capital. The increment to production, which is called the marginal product of capital MPK, takes place at the beginning of period t, is stored without cost during the period, and is sold at the beginning of period $t+1$ for $p(MPK)$ where p denotes the (assumed for now) constant price of output. If ρ is the required rate of return for investors, then the present value of the net cash flow follows from just adding up the pieces:

present value of net cash flow from the machine =
$$-q_t - \delta q_t + [pMPK_{t+1} + q_{t+1}]/(1 + \rho). \qquad (2\text{--}1)$$

With decreasing returns, the firm will continue to purchase machines until the last machine just pays for itself; that is, until the above equation equals zero at the margin. Thus, for the marginal investment, the cost of capital is

$$pMPK_{t+1} = q_t[\rho + \delta + \rho\delta - (\Delta q_{t+1}/q_t)] \qquad (2\text{--}2)$$

where $\Delta q_{t+1}/q_t$ denotes the capital gain or loss on the asset because of a change in its market price.[1]

While ignoring the small interaction term $\rho\delta$, the firm's cost of capital in use has three components: the first is the combined real cost of debt and equity financing, ρq_t, which incorporates the required real rate of return to bondholders and shareholders, each after personal taxes; the second is the economic rate of decay of the capital with an unchanging relative price of new capital, δq_t; and the third is an offset due to an instantaneous real capital gain on the capital, Δq. Assuming diminishing returns, then the marginal product of capital decreases as more capital is purchased, so the demand for capital is inversely related to the user cost. If the required rate of return is in part determined by the interest rate, then the demand for capital will go up when interest rates go down. This formula is easily modified to include taxes on profits, as well as subsidies to capital such as an investment tax credit. When this is done, it is easy to show today's user cost of capital:

$$C_t = q_t(\rho + \delta - \Delta q/q)(1 - \tau_c z)/(1 - \tau_c) \qquad (2\text{-}3)$$

where τ_c is the corporate tax rate and z is the depreciation rate.

Derived by Hall and Jorgenson (1967), this familiar formula draws on the seminal work of Jorgenson (1963). The introduction of corporate taxes affects the user cost of capital in two ways. First, in the absence of tax deductions for depreciation and interest costs, an increase in the corporate income tax rate, τ_c, increases the before-tax marginal product of capital necessary to yield an acceptable after-tax rate of return to investors and thereby increases the user cost. Second, a higher tax rate of corporate income increases the value of depreciation deductions and hence reduces the user cost. The multiplicative factor, $(1 - \tau_c z)/(1 - \tau_c)$, captures the combination of these two effects: on balance, user cost is increased under current U.S. tax law because expensing—or the immediate write-off—of plant and equipment expenditures is not permitted (that is, $z < 1$). [2]

Early Empirical Results

Jorgenson (1963) investigated whether this theory could be used to describe aggregate fluctuations in U.S. investment. Moving from this equilibrium relationship to an empirical model, however, required a few more steps. Because the choice of capital determines output, the theory does not relate capital to a set of exogenous variables.[3] Rather, it expresses a relationship between endogenous variables that holds in equilibrium. Indeed, given an assumption about the technology that turns capital into output, the theory does not define an investment relationship, that is, the flow of capital, but rather describes only the equilibrium stock of capital.[4] Jorgenson moved to an investment specification by defining a firm's desired capital stock, K^*, as output divided by the user cost, Y/c, and then assuming that the firm gradually approached this desired stock over time. He assumed that the rate (ω) at which the firm closed the gap between its actual and desired stocks was given exogenously and did not affect the level of the desired stock. These assumptions yielded the estimating equation:

$$I_t = \sum_{i=0}^{T} \omega_i (K_{t-i} - K^*_{t-1-i}) + \delta K_{t-1}. \qquad (2\text{--}4)$$

Hall and Jorgenson (1967) originally used such a model to explain aggregate investment and concluded that it described the data well. Eisner and his collaborators later pointed out that the model they estimated—recognizing that K^* was the ratio of output to the user cost—could be capturing accelerator effects, which had long been known as strong explanatory factors for investment. In particular, if one constrained the user cost to be a constant, one could rewrite equation 2–4 as

$$I_t = \sum_{i=0}^{T} \omega_{i,uc} (Y_{t-i} - Y_{t-1-i}) + \delta K_{t-1}, \qquad (2\text{--}5)$$

which is a form of an accelerator model. When critics of Hall and Jorgenson isolated the separate contribution of the user cost to explaining investment, they found the effect of user cost negligible (see Eisner 1969, 1970; Eisner and Nadiri 1968; and Chirinko and Eisner 1983); that is, equation 2–5 does just as good a job describing investment as equation 2–4.

Subsequently, while the neoclassical school may have held the theoretical high ground, the empirical implementations of neoclassical models using time-series data have not succeeded. The time-series evidence has always revealed that lags of output are highly correlated with investment, but interest rates and tax variables have generally provided limited additional explanatory power. Models emphasizing the net return to investing are defeated in forecasting "horse races" by ad hoc models, and structural variables are frequently found to be economically or statistically insignificant.[5]

As the negative evidence mounted, many economists became convinced that interest rates, taxes, and the other components of user cost do not help predict investment behavior, because firms do not pay attention to these variables. Indeed, few corporate decision-makers anecdotally cite user cost as an important concern when evaluating investment projects. If the tests were correct, then the ability of government policy to affect investment would be highly questionable.

Thus, by the late 1960s, the neoclassical model developed by Jorgenson and others had become the standard model for studying the response of investment to tax policy. This situation presented economists with a problem. On the one hand, the neoclassical approach offers a theoretical link between tax policy parameters—the corporate tax rate, the present value of depreciation allowances, and the investment tax credit—and investment through the user cost of capital.[6] On the other hand, the empirical evidence suggested that the more rigorous theory did not improve the econometrician's ability to explain aggregate investment fluctuations or the response of business investment to changes in tax policy. Indeed, the tax policy variable had no effect at all on investment.

The Challenge and the First Wave of Responses

These facts presented two challenges to economists who believed that the empirical evidence was somehow flawed. First, a theory was needed to describe why yesterday's output is so important, even though any investment benefit will occur in the future. Second, a coherent story had to explain why investment could respond to changes in interest rates and tax rates and yet appear not to in time-series data. This section summarizes efforts to address the first challenge; the following section turns to the second.

Motivated by the hope that the simplest neoclassical models failed to explain investment fluctuations because they were too stylized, economists devoted substantial energy to extending these models to incorporate more realistic assumptions in the 1970s and early 1980s.[7] By the late 1980s, they had made substantial progress in addressing the first of the two challenges. The biggest step occurred when theorists explicitly incorporated costs of adjusting the capital stock into their models. According to these new theories, if firms attempt to make huge wholesale changes in their production technologies overnight, they face enormous costs—costs that are significantly lowered if the firms change the capital stock gradually. This new assumption provides a link—absent in the first neoclassical models—between what the firm was doing yesterday and what it plans to do tomorrow. According to these new models, investment is forward-looking and is based on rational expectations of future variables that affect profit at the margin, but investment also depends on how much capital is already on hand. Because firms base their expectations of future variables in part on their observations of the past, researchers identified a link between numerous lagged variables and current investment. Anything that helps predict future market conditions might matter in investment regressions. Thus, the correlation of past output growth and future fundamentals could be used to rationalize a strong correlation between current investment and past values of the growth of output.

The new investment models emphasizing the net return to investment, but with adjustment costs, have yielded four complementary empirical representations. Each begins with the firm maximizing its net present value. The first-order conditions for investment and capital lead to a Euler equation describing the period-to-period optimal path of investment. Investment today depends on prices, taxes, interest rates, and expected investment. Abel and Blanchard (1986) solved the Euler equation and developed an estimating equation that relates investment to its expected current and future marginal revenue products of capital. Alternatively, effects of tax parameters may be estimated from the Euler equation itself (see, for example, Abel 1980 and Hubbard and Kashyap 1992). As in Auerbach 1983b and Abel 1990, investment can be expressed in terms of current and future values of the user cost of capital and, under some conditions, expressed in terms of average Q, which is the market value of the firm divided by the replacement cost of capital. This approach was suggested initially by Tobin (1969), with the necessary conditions supplied by Hayashi (1982).

Models based on the Q representation of the firm's investment problem occupied much of the empirical research by the 1980s.[8] One reason for the popularity of the model is certainly its intuitive appeal. Suppose Q for some firm (ignoring taxes) equals 1.5. For only $100, this firm can buy a machine that the market values at $150. The firm can sell shares and buy machines until the value of a new machine in the stock market declines all the way to the cost of purchasing that machine. Alternatively, if a firm has a Q of 0.8, then the market values the machines held by that company at less than the replacement cost. A $100 machine inside the company is worth only $80. If the firm sells a machine, it will raise $100, and so the firm makes its shareholders better off by selling machines. The firm should continue to sell machines until the stock market value of a machine inside the firm equals its replacement cost. Another key appeal of the Q approach was that it related investment to a variable that under certain assumptions was easier to observe than the user cost of capital.

When asked to explain the time-series movements of investment, however, these new models proved disappointing as well. The basic accelerator model, which depends only on output, did just as well as, if not better than, the Q theory in forecasting horse races. Moreover, parameter estimates for the new models tended to be wildly implausible. The coefficient on Q, for example, indicates the speed with which firms can adjust their investment to its target or optimal level. If the Q coefficient is inconsequential, then investment does not respond quickly to Q values different from 1. The negligible Q coefficient reported in the literature often implied that the costs of adjustment incurred when installing a new machine were larger than the purchase price of the machine itself.

Researchers usually estimated such models with either ordinary-least-squares (OLS) or generalized method-of-moments (GMM) techniques with instrumental variables. Cummins, Hassett, and Hubbard (1994, 1996) note that the tiny conventional estimated values of the coefficient on Q, ranging from 0.01 to 0.05, in firm-level panel data for the United States or for other countries imply marginal costs of adjustment of $1–5 per dollar of investment. Such estimates, which have emerged in many empirical studies (see, for example,

Summers 1981, Salinger and Summers 1983, and Fazzari, Hubbard, and Petersen 1988), imply insignificant effects of permanent investment incentives on investment. Applications of the alternative approaches to time-series data, while promising, continued to suffer by comparison with accelerator models.

This work completed the first wave of responses to the neoclassical failure. The second wave of responses explored the alternative specifications with the use of much richer data sources than had generally been used. Before discussing these contributions, the next section presents several charts that confirm the results of the time-series literature.

Lessons from the Time-Series Data

Figure 2–1 plots aggregate U.S. equipment investment against several investment fundamentals. The top panel shows the co-movement of investment and the user cost of capital. The two series rarely move together in an obvious way, and the correlation since 1960 is a statistically insignificant −0.11. The second panel illustrates the strong co-movements between investment and corporate cash flow. These two series are roughly coincident, and the correlation over time is a highly significant 0.64. The bottom panel illustrates the accelerator effect, which relates changes in the growth rates of output and equipment spending. As with cash flow, the correlation is large and highly significant, and the coincidence of the series is visually striking.

While one should be cautious in interpreting such correlations formally, they nonetheless suggest clear patterns. Aggregate equipment investment varies significantly over the business cycle; it neither lags nor leads the cycle; and it is highly correlated with other variables that are also highly procyclical. The time-series correlation between investment and the user cost,

FIGURE 2–1
FUNDAMENTAL DETERMINANTS OF EQUIPMENT INVESTMENT, 1960–1995

User Cost of Capital

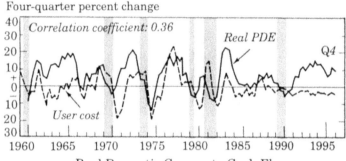

Real Domestic Corporate Cash Flow

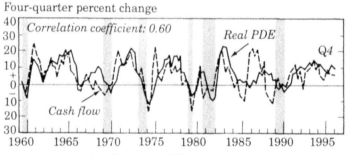

Acceleration of Business Output

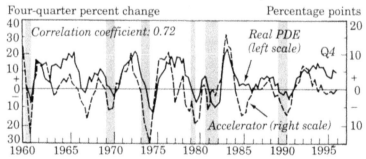

NOTE: The accelerator is the eight-quarter percent change in business output less the year-earlier eight-quarter percent change.
SOURCE: Author's calculations.

on the other hand, is quite weak. Figure 2–1 can be
thought of as a visual summary of the early investment
literature: accelerator effects are strong and obvious;
user-cost effects appear weaker and more subtle.
I focus on studies of equipment investment, in large
part because empirical attempts to model investment
in structures have been more disappointing. Figure 2–
2, which repeats figure 2–1 with the relevant fundamentals related to the growth rate of investment in
nonresidential structures, illustrates this problem.
Structures investment is less clearly correlated with
all the fundamentals. The correlation with user cost is
insignificant and has the incorrect sign; the correlation
with cash flow is about one-fourth of that between cash
flow and equipment investment; and the accelerator
effect, while still noticeable, is significantly weaker.

An alternative branch of the investment literature
has followed the suggestion of Tobin (1969) that investment should be related to Q, the ratio of the market
value of the firm to the replacement costs of its capital
stock. Figure 2–3 depicts the correlation of aggregate
business fixed investment with Q.[9] The top panel com-
pares the level of real investment with the level of Q.
Clearly, the low-frequency movements in the two series
are not highly correlated. The bottom panel relates the
growth rates of these two series. Here it appears that
growth in Q leads growth in investment somewhat, although the relationship is weak, and the contemporaneous correlation is actually negative.[10]

Does this mean that the neoclassical model is dead?
Recent researchers have argued that movements of aggregate variables—including investment—are determined simultaneously and that disentangling the
marginal impact of a single driving variable is difficult,
if not impossible, with time-series data. Suppose, for
example, that aggregate demand increases exogenously
for some reason. This shift might lead firms to be more
optimistic about their sales prospects and to purchase

FIGURE 2–2
FUNDAMENTAL DETERMINANTS OF NRS SPENDING, 1960–1995

NRS Cost of Capital

Four-quarter percent change

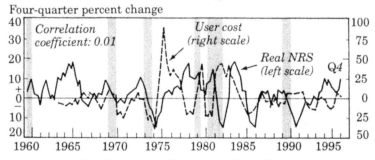

Real Domestic Corporate Cash Flow

Four-quarter percent change

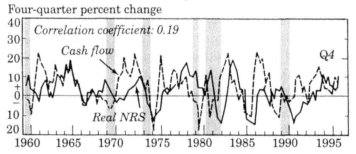

Acceleration of Business Output

Four-quarter percent change   Percentage points

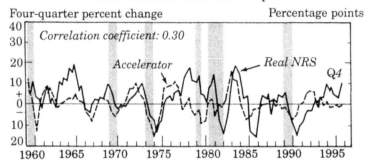

NOTE: The accelerator is the eight-quarter percent change in business output less the year-earlier eight-quarter percent change.
SOURCE: Author's calculations.

FIGURE 2–3
TOBIN'S *Q* AND THE *I/K* RATIO, 1960–1996
(index: 1987 = 100)

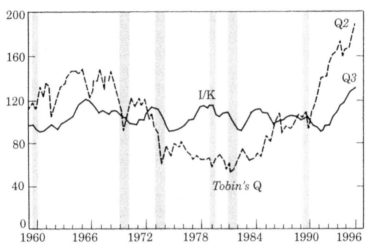

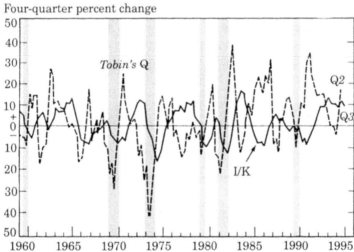

SOURCE: Author's calculations.

more investment goods; the change might also be expected—at least in the short run—to lead to higher interest rates. Examining the correlation between investment and the interest rate might even reveal that the sign is the opposite of the theory' s prediction. While an instrumental variables procedure might allow for overcoming this simultaneity problem, the estimator is only as good as the instruments. It is difficult, however, to imagine an appropriate set of instruments for this application.

In summary, the tendency for several aggregate variables to move together over the business cycle makes it difficult to isolate effects of individual fundamentals on investment when using time-series data. Even if investment is responsive to tax policy, it might not appear so in the aggregate data, since so many other important determinants of investment are moving over the business cycle as well. Hence, an approach of partial-equilibrium investment demand might have scant power to explain aggregate investment fluctuations. Microeconomic data, however, provide a rich additional source of variation. I now turn to the microdata studies.

3

New Identification Strategies

Data, then, do not appear to favor neoclassical models over accelerator models in part because of a problem of simultaneous equations. If, on the one hand, the data were dominated by exogenous increases or decreases in the real interest rate, then the user-cost movements would lead investment to decrease or increase, respectively. If, on the other hand, investment rises with positive vigor, then higher investment demand puts upward pressure on the real interest rate. Hence, to the extent that data incorporate exogenous changes both in the real interest rate and in the intercept of the investment function, the positive relationship between investment and the user cost of capital due to shifts in the investment function may dominate the hypothesized negative relationship between investment and the user cost of capital. In this case, the estimated coefficient on the user cost of capital will be too small and lead to estimated adjustment costs that are too large. Such simultaneity increases apparent accelerator effects, because positive shifts of the investment function raise both investment and output. Controlling for these effects has been the goal of the second wave of the literature, which is discussed below.

Using Cross-Sectional Variation
to Identify Tax Effects

As noted, the use of instrumental variables remedies this simultaneity problem in the estimation of neoclassical models. Conventional instrumental variables (including lagged endogenous variables or sales-to-capital ratios) have not proved helpful. Major tax reforms arguably offer periods in which there is exogenous cross-sectional variation in the user cost of capital or tax-adjusted Q. Auerbach and Hassett (1991) and Cummins, Hassett, and Hubbard (1994, 1996) demonstrate that major tax reforms are also associated with significant firm- and asset-level variation in key tax parameters (such as the effective rate of investment tax credit and the present value of depreciation allowances). Hence, tax variables are likely to be a good instrument for user cost or Q during tax reforms.

The variation across assets is large within most years, as is the time-series variation. In addition, the relative treatment of different assets changes somewhat over time. Following the removal of the investment tax credit and the reduction of the corporate tax rate by the Tax Reform Act of 1986, for example, the cross-sectional variation across assets fell, consistent with the act's stated goal to level the playing field.

Focusing on the Tax Reform Act of 1986, Auerbach and Hassett (1991) found similar coefficients with asset-level data and cross-sectional variation in the user cost. Using contemporaneous tax variables during major tax reforms, Cummins, Hassett, and Hubbard (1994) estimate the coefficient on Q as 0.65 for the United States, compared with a paltry 0.048 under conventional estimates. They obtained similar estimates for each of the other major U.S. tax reforms in the postwar period with data from Compustat. Cummins, Hassett, and Hubbard (1995) use vector autoregressions to forecast investment in the year following a tax reform and then compare the forecast errors for each of the assets with the changes in the user cost for that asset. The forecast errors for investment should be negatively correlated with forecast errors for the user cost of capital if firms know that the changes are coming, but these changes cannot be forecast with simple linear regression techniques. For example, if a firm knows that this year its user cost will increase sharply, the firm will lower its investment. If a forecaster does not know about the increase in user cost, he will make a large forecasting error. The authors find a clear negative correlation in these surprises.

Table 3–1 shows the significance of using exogenous tax changes to identify changes in Q.[11] Taken from Cummins, Hassett, and Hubbard (1996), the table presents estimates of a simple equation relating the ratio of investment to capital to Tobin's Q during major tax reforms in fourteen countries during the 1980s; firm-level data are taken from Compustat's Global Vantage.

As discussed below, empirical researchers have offered three general explanations of the failure to estimate significant tax effects on investment: (1) measurement error in fundamental variables, (2) misspecification of costs of adjusting the capital stock, and (3) capital stock heterogeneity. All three research programs have contributed to an understanding of the responsiveness of investment to changes in the net return to investing and have reached similar conclusions about the likely effects of tax policy for some important cases.

Measurement Error in Fundamental Variables

As long acknowledged, measurement error in Q or the user cost of capital may bias downward the estimated coefficient. An important recent note (Goolsbee 1998b)

TABLE 3-1
ESTIMATES OF TAX-ADJUSTED Q MODEL
FOR FOURTEEN COUNTRIES

Country	Conventional Panel Data Estimated Coefficient on Q	Estimated Coefficient with Contemporaneous Tax Instruments
Australia	0.050	0.289
	(0.019)	(0.153)
Belgium	0.103	0.587
	(0.044)	(0.422)
Canada	0.041	0.521
	(0.009)	(0.127)
Denmark	0.104	0.765
	(0.085)	(0.308)
France	0.085	0.388
	(0.042)	(0.116)
Germany	0.095	0.784
	(0.040)	(0.296)
Italy	0.051	0.180
	(0.018)	(0.120)
Japan	0.029	0.086
	(0.008)	(0.035)
Netherlands	0.069	0.633
	(0.044)	(0.150)
Norway	0.069	0.512
	(0.031)	(0.295)
Spain	0.044	0.404
	(0.028)	(0.233)
Sweden	0.051	0.293
	(0.047)	(0.169)
United Kingdom	0.062	0.589
	(0.013)	(0.078)
United States	0.048	0.650
	(0.006)	(0.077)

NOTE: The dependent variable is I/K. For column 1, see table 5 in Cummins, Hassett, and Hubbard 1996 for GMM estimates. Instruments include twice- and thrice-lagged values of Q, (I/K), and the ratios of cash flow to capital. For column 2, see table 7 in Cummins, Hassett, and Hubbard 1996 for GMM estimates. Instruments include twice- and thrice-lagged values of I/K and the ratio of cash flow to capital, twice-lagged value nontax components of q, and contemporaneous values of tax parameters.

SOURCE: Calculations in Cummins, Hassett, and Hubbard 1996 with Global Vantage data.

has documented that measurement error is indeed important. Several alternative techniques have been suggested to address this measurement error, including (1) making statistical corrections, (2) avoiding the use of Q or representations of user cost, (3) using new proxies for Q, (4) focusing on periods or frequencies in which firm variation in fundamental variables is less subject to measurement error, and (5) modifying assumptions about the financial tensions faced by businesses. Each possibility is considered in turn.

At least two problems in measuring Q might affect estimated adjustment costs. First, to the extent that the stock market is excessively volatile, Q might not reflect market fundamentals. Second, the replacement value of the capital stock in the denominator of Q is likely to be measured with error. Griliches and Hausman (1986) argue that measurement error will lead to different biases among potential estimators that are similar in that they control for firm-specific effects but differ in their signal-to-noise ratios; this situation makes it possible to place bounds on the importance of measurement error. Cummins, Hassett, and Hubbard (1994) estimate a Q model by using first differences and longer differences (as opposed to the conventional fixed-effects, within-group estimator) to address problems of measurement error. Their estimated adjustment costs decline significantly with the long differences.

In a time-series setting, Caballero (1994) pursues an alternative estimation strategy based on a suggestion by Stock and Watson (1993). Caballero argues that small-sample biases of typically employed time-series estimation procedures are particularly severe when estimating adjustment cost models, and he shows that elasticities will generally be biased down. Using the procedure of Stock and Watson for estimating the low-frequency relationships between variables in small samples, Caballero estimates a long-run elasticity of investment regarding the user cost of approximate unity. This is much larger than the early estimates but roughly consistent with the other studies summarized in this section. Another approach departs from the strategy of using proxies for marginal Q and relies on the firm's Euler equation to model the investment decision. As long as one makes the same assumption about technology and adjustment costs, the Euler equation can be derived from the same model as the conventional Q or user cost of capital models. By not relying on the representation of investment function, one can sidestep problems of measuring marginal Q.

Tests following this approach have frequently used panel data on manufacturing firms to estimate the Euler equation (Pindyck and Rotemberg 1983; Shapiro 1986; Gilchrist 1991; Whited 1992; Bond and Meghir 1994; and Hubbard, Kashyap, and Whited 1995). Studies using Compustat data for the United States cannot reject the frictionless neoclassical model for most firms, and the parameters for the estimated adjustment cost are more reasonable than those found in estimates of Q models. Hubbard, Kashyap, and Whited (1995), for example, report Q-coefficient estimates between 1.0 and 2.2. Cummins, Harris, and Hassett (1995) report similar estimates for European manufacturing firms, and Cummins and Hubbard (1995), for investment in overseas subsidiaries of U.S. multinational corporations.

The measure of average Q used as a proxy for marginal Q in most empirical studies is constructed as the ratio of the market value of the financial claims on the firm (equity and debt) to the replacement cost of the firm's capital stock. The third approach bypasses using financial variables as proxies for marginal Q by forecasting the expected present value of the current and future profits generated by an incremental unit of capital, that is, the expected value of marginal Q—an idea developed by Abel and Blanchard (1986) and applied to panel data by Gilchrist and Himmelberg (1995).

Using such an approach, Gilchrist and Himmelberg (1995) report estimates of adjustment costs that are roughly consistent with the Euler equation estimates discussed above. In addition, they test whether cash flow is an independent fundamental variable explaining investment and find that it is for a subset of firms that are likely to face liquidity constraints.[12] A discussion of this latter result follows.

Tax reforms are not the only plausible reform that can be used to estimate adjustment costs. Much evidence suggests that the power of unions to expropriate returns is significant and that the "union tax" adjusts as the return to capital changes. If union wage demands vary with the return to capital, then the union rent share is—in part at least—a tax on capital, distorting the level of investment when it is introduced, and union certification elections are analogous to tax increases in their likely impact on investment. Fallick and Hassett (forthcoming) explore whether a change in the union status of the firm is another type of large identifiable shock that affects purchases of capital. Using firm-level panel data, they document a large negative response of investment to affirmative elections on union certification. In their sample, for most firms that experience union certification elections, net investment turns significantly negative in the year immediately following the election, with the mean response to union certification being roughly the same as if—given the responsiveness of investment to user cost in Cummins, Hassett, and Hubbard 1994—the corporate tax rate were increased thirty-five percentage points. This evidence is consistent with the neoclassical view that shocks to marginal profitability significantly affect investment decisions.

In summary, various empirical implementations of the neoclassical model with convex adjustment costs have attempted to mitigate measurement error and other econometric problems in conventional OLS and GMM estimates by using panel data. The methods generally yield estimates that imply marginal costs of adjustment of approximately $0.10 per dollar of additional investment (using the estimate in Cummins, Hassett, and Hubbard 1995 as a benchmark) and elasticities of investment regarding user cost of capital between –0.5 and –1.0.

Misspecification of Adjustment Costs

The empirical studies just mentioned accept the conventional belief that costs of adjusting capital stock are convex. The Q, user cost of capital, and Euler equation approaches can all be derived from the same intertemporal maximization problem, given common assumptions about technology, competition, and adjustment costs. An important recent line of inquiry focuses on modeling and testing the effects of irreversibility and uncertainty on firms' investment decisions (see, for example, the excellent survey by Dixit and Pindyck 1994).[13] If this literature is correct, then there may be important regions in which tax policy has little or no effect on investment; knowledge of which region an economy currently exists in is an important prerequisite to any policy analysis. Finally, these models might explain a key remaining puzzle in the literature; that is, why firms report in surveys that they use such high threshold rates (see Summers 1987).

Neoclassical models implicitly assume an efficient secondary market for capital; hence, irreversibility poses no problem. If a firm purchases a machine today and the output market turns sour, the firm can recoup the purchase price of the machine at that time. The neoclassical primer made exactly that assumption. If, however, investment is irreversible, then the firm faces the chance that it will not be able to sell the machine. In this setup, there is a gain from delaying investment and allowing the random price process to move either far enough above the neoclassical breakeven point that the probability of the bad state becomes low or to the point where purchasing the machine clearly does not make sense. An investment extinguishes the value of the call option of delay, an option that has positive value when prices are uncertain. In this approach, the value of the lost option is a component of the opportunity cost of investment. In the terminology of the Q framework, the threshold criterion for investment requires that marginal Q exceed unity by the value of maintaining the call option to invest. As a consequence, corporate managers making investment decisions may require high threshold rates.

Indeed, at least part of the interest in option-based investment models has been raised by a problem in many time-series studies: the response of investment to changes in Q or the user cost of capital is implausibly small and thus perhaps implies that in some regions Q varies but investment does not. In addition, it is not difficult to suggest examples of nonconvex adjustment costs, such as retooling in automobile plants or the adoption of more energy-efficient kilns in cement plants.

Abel and Eberly (1995) provide a general framework that encompasses irreversibility, fixed costs, and a wide array of alternative adjustment cost specifications. They show that under certain conditions the investment behavior of firms can be characterized by three distinct regimes: (1) gross investment is positive; (2) gross investment is zero; and (3) gross investment is negative. The responsiveness of investment to fundamentals differs across regimes. Abel and Eberly's more general model predicts a region in which gross investment will stay at zero for a range of unfavorable values of Q. Because this model nests the more traditional Q models, it provides a useful empirical framework.

Researchers are beginning to study the impact of alternative assumptions of adjustment cost within structural investment models with panel data. Barnett and Sakellaris (1995) use Compustat data to investigate the implication of the Abel and Eberly (1995) model that investment alternates between regimes of insensitivity to Q and regimes of responsiveness to Q. The region of inactivity should be close to the region with predicted negative investment. Because the thresholds for these regions are unknown, conventional asymptotic distributions do not apply. Barnett and Sakellaris use a statistical framework that allows them to estimate the threshold points and the coefficients on Q simultaneously in the different regions given the threshold points. They find evidence of a nonlinear relationship between investment and Q; in particular, they estimate the greatest responsiveness of investment to Q for low values of Q and the smallest for high values of Q. On average, they estimate that the elasticity of investment pertaining to Q is about unity but that the aggregate elasticity varies considerably over time, depending on the average level of Q. Barnett and Sakellaris argue that their results imply that adjustment cost may not be quadratic: the most likely cause is not the inability of firms to disinvest, but rather their reluctance to make major changes.

Barnett and Sakellaris's results are not necessarily inconsistent with the measurement error story. Some firms in their Compustat universe have values of average Q that are astronomical, presumably because the capital stock measure is missing important components of goodwill or human capital. If one accepts that Q is a poor measure of fundamentals for these firms, then the result that investment does not respond as much to Q for these firms is not surprising. In the more typical range of Q values, the investment response seems to accord well with the predictions of the convex model for adjustment cost.

Cummins, Hassett, and Oliner (1998) use nonparametric estimation to fit a nonlinear Q model and find, like Barnett and Sakellaris, that investment increases with Q sharply for lower values of Q and then increases far less sharply for higher values of Q. They use analysts' earnings forecasts to attempt to correct for problems of measurement error but find that this step does not change the curvature of the investment-Q function.

Further Use of Adjustment Costs. Caballero, Engel, and Haltiwanger (1995) explore adjustment costs in a more general framework. Using a subset of 7,000 U.S. manufacturing plants from the Census Bureau's Longitudinal Research Database (LRD), they explore whether cross-sectional patterns of investment are consistent with symmetric, convex models of adjustment cost or whether the data imply that there are nonconvexities.[14] Caballero, Engel, and Haltiwanger proceed in two steps. First, they assume that there are no adjustment costs and that the Jorgensonian model adequately describes a firm's desired capital stock (K^*).[15] They then compare in each period a firm's beginning-of-period capital stock with its desired stock and call the difference $(K^* - K_{t-1})$ "mandated investment." Second, they explore how firms actually adjust their capital stocks. In this step they find that the relationship between actual and mandated investment is highly nonlinear. If mandated investment is negative, then firms do not quickly adjust their capital stocks downward. If mandated investment is small and positive, then firms do not respond much. If mandated investment is large, then firms adjust their capital stocks quickly. The researchers conclude that a kinky adjustment or (S, s) model—in which firms have a range of inaction and adjust their capital stocks to their desired levels only when the gap between current and desired capital stock is large enough—offers a good description of the data. Doyle and Whited (1998) provide important additional evidence suggesting that the (S, s) model may provide an important microfoundation for future macroinvestment work. The authors explore the relationship between deviations of optimal from actual capital across industries and the proportion of industry risk that is idiosyncratic, a relationship first explored by Bertola and Caballero (1990). They show that in (S, s) models this ratio is negatively correlated with persistence in industry aggregate deviations from optimal capital. That is, if most shocks are idiosyncratic in a given industry, then the shocks will cancel out at the industry level, and the frictionless model may be a reasonable description of aggregate fluctuations in that industry. If most shocks affect the industry as a whole, then the industry might look like an individual (S, s) firm, with highly persistent deviations of actual from desired capital. Doyle and Whited construct a measure of risk and industry measures of capital and show that the more idiosyncratic the risk in an industry, the more fleeting are the deviations from optimal aggregated capital. This important evidence suggests that the traditional-style models may do a poor job describing short-run dynamics that surround tax reforms.

Goolsbee and Gross (1997), in analyzing aircraft replacement by airlines, find clear evidence of nonconvexities, with firms demonstrating an area of inaction but with adjustment costs conditional on making an investment apparently quadratic. They show that aggregation obscures the nonconvexities and biases upward estimates of adjustment costs.

Using firm-level data from Compustat, Abel and Eberly (1996) estimate that the relationship between investment and fundamental determinants (Q and the tax-adjusted price of capital goods) is concave; that is, the response of investment to fundamental determinants is positive but monotonically declining. Abel and Eberly's results suggest that the distribution of tax-adjusted Q or the user cost of capital may be a determinant of aggregate investment. The caution that applied to Barnett and Sakellaris's conclusions, however, applies here as well: large observed values of Q may not coincide with high levels of investment because the high Q values reflect mismeasurement rather than extraordinary fundamentals.

Caballero, Engel, and Haltiwanger also illustrate how to construct aggregate implications from their microeconomic results. Integrating over the microeconomic distribution of plants, they calculate a predicted aggregate elasticity of investment regarding the user cost of capital. The estimates of this elasticity vary considerably over time. If, on the one hand, many plants are near the region for which mandated investment is huge, then small changes in the user cost can greatly affect an aggregate investment. If, on the other hand, the bulk of the distribution of mandated investment is in the region of low responsiveness of investment to fundamentals, then changes in the user cost will have little impact. The researchers agree with the main conclusion of Cummins, Hassett, and Hubbard (1994) that the aggregate elasticity of investment regarding user cost is between –0.5 and –1.0 and also conclude that tax reforms apparently have had large effects on investment. They caution, however, that the reforms have had such effects because they coincidentally occurred during periods in which the plant-level distribution of mandated investment was aligned to allow a large effect of changes in tax parameters. This would happen if, for example, investment tax credits were removed in booms, when mandated investment is enormous and an increase in user cost can cause firms to cancel significant investment plans. As a consequence, Caballero, Engel, and Haltiwanger argue that researchers must consult the microdistribution of mandated investment before predicting the likely impact of future tax reforms on business investment.[16]

Alternatively, Cummins, Hassett, and Hubbard (1994, 1996) argue that recovering reasonable estimates of the response of investment to Q or the user cost of capital is easiest when large exogenous changes in the distribution of structural determinants occur, as during tax reforms. In answer to the alternative interpretation that firms respond only to large changes in fundamentals, Cummins, Hassett, and Hubbard use firm-level data to discover evidence of the bunching of investment around tax reforms. They estimate transition probabilities among various ranges of I/K over the year before, the year of, and the year after tax reform and find no evidence that firms with large investments were likely to have lower investment in prior or subsequent years. Indeed, only a tiny fraction of the sample was ever found to transit from high-investment to low-investment states.

In part, the conclusions of these studies may differ because of differences in the level of aggregation. At a sufficiently fine level of disaggregation, all investment looks lumpy. The plant-level evidence suggests that investment appears lumpy, but the firm-level evidence does not corroborate this. There may be interesting differences between the investment behavior of plants and firms, if, for example, managerial attention is limited and only a fraction of a firm's plants adjust their capital in a given year. Clearly, reconciling the plant-level and firm-level results is an important topic for future research.

Heterogeneity of Capital Stock

Recently, Cummins and Dey (1998) and Goolsbee (1998b) opened up a promising alternative path. Cummins and

Dey argue that studies of investment behavior have largely ignored capital heterogeneity. They estimate a dynamic structural model in which different types of capital are interrelated in both the production and the adjustment-cost technologies. Thus, if a plant is shut down for installation of new machines, then structural alterations might as well be performed at the same time. This interrelationship produces a bunching of investment similar to that suggested by models of irreversibility. Applied to data on publicly traded U.S. firms, taken from Compustat, their results help explain some empirical failings of the neoclassical model. Cummins and Dey also show that when capital heterogeneity is ignored, estimates of adjustment costs are biased upward and estimates of factor substitution in production are biased downward.

Goolsbee (1998b) argues that tax subsidies will change the relative price of high-quality capital if high quality is interpreted to mean that the machine requires less future maintenance. Changes in the quality of machines could in principle significantly alter perceptions concerning the effects of tax reform. In particular, Goolsbee shows that tax reforms appear to be associated empirically with major changes in the quality of machines purchased. To the extent that deflators do not adequately account for quality adjustments, perceptions about the effects of policy may be inaccurate.

Summing Up

Recent studies appear to have reached a consensus that the elasticity of investment regarding the user cost of capital is between −0.5 and −1.0. Recent studies using convex costs of adjustment and using nonconvex costs of adjustment agree that the long-run elasticity of investment to the user cost is high by the standards of the early empirical literature. This range of estimated responses of investment to tax parameters is well above the consensus of only a few years earlier and suggests that investment tax policy can significantly affect the path of aggregate capital formation. One should be cautious, however, in moving from the microeconomic evidence to aggregate predictions. Caballero, Engel, and Haltiwanger (1995) demonstrate a technique for aggregating the microdistribution of firms to calculate aggregate investment demand, but little is known about the general equilibrium effects of major policy changes.

4
Arguments for and against Lowering Taxes on Capital

Having shown that tax incentives for investment are important components of the net return to investing and that the long-term responses of investment to permanent tax incentives are large, I now turn to the deeper policy question of permanent incentives for investment even if such incentives increase the stock of business fixed capital. The question of the desirability of short-run incentives is then addressed. Economists generally argue against intervention. Under what circumstances might one advocate distortionary investment incentives?

Tax Reform Today Could Remove Distortion

Under current law, taxes increase the user cost of capital by about 10 percent. The extension of the expensing of capital investments would remove distortions associated with the current tax system. Indeed, the removal of capital distortions provides the most powerful growth effects of flat-tax proposals. One could easily design an investment incentive system with the same effect.

Optimal tax theory generally suggests that it is

never optimal to distort production decisions. Thus, optimal tax theory would support the imposition of a fairly generous investment tax credit onto the current system. Judd (1995) has advanced another argument for subsidies to equipment investment. He concludes that the optimal tax on equipment investment is negative. In Judd's model, capital-goods–producing industries are imperfectly competitive, and equipment prices contain significant markups.[17] These markups are analogous to tax distortions. Tax credits can return a firm's input mixture to the optimal social level if the government designs investment subsidies that equate the prices paid for different types of equipment to marginal cost.

Investment Incentives Are Bad Because of Interasset Distortions

In practice, investment tax credits have generally been applicable only to investments in equipment. One argument against such credits is that they introduce interasset distortions. If these interasset distortions are large enough, then any gain from removing the intertemporal distortion from the higher capital income tax might be squandered.

Auerbach (1989b) developed a model to study this issue. His model has a multifactor production technology that allows for substitution between labor and three different types of capital (equipment, structures, and land), on the one hand, and nine production sectors (agriculture; mining; construction; durable goods manufacturing; nondurable goods manufacturing; transportation, communication, and utilities; wholesale and retail trade; finance, insurance, and real estate; and other services), on the other. Auerbach finds that across a wide array of parameter values, the interasset distortion from nonneutral capital income taxation is surprisingly small.

One should not conclude from Auerbach's results that differential taxation is desired. Rather, if one expects that political forces will push a tax reform in the direction of introducing interasset distortions, one should conclude from Auerbach's work that the negative effects of these distortions are not likely to be large enough to negate the likely positive effects of lower capital taxes.

Failure of Investment Incentives Because of Liquidity Constraints

If liquidity constrains a firm, it can invest only up to the amount of cash on hand. In contrast to the frictionless capital markets in the standard neoclassical model considered to this point, earlier applied research on investment, especially the work of Meyer and Kuh (1957), stressed the significance of financial considerations (particularly internal funds or net worth) for business investment. Since the mid-1960s, however, most applied research on investment isolated the real decisions of a firm from financing. The intellectual justification for this shift in approach drew on the seminal work by Modigliani and Miller (1958), who demonstrated the irrelevance of financial structure and financial policy for real investment decisions under certain conditions. The central Modigliani-Miller conclusion, which facilitated the early development of the neoclassical model, was that a firm's financial structure will not affect its value in frictionless capital markets. As a result, if their assumptions are satisfied, real firm decisions, motivated by the maximization of shareholders' claims, are independent of financial factors such as the availability of internal funds.

The assumption of representative firms (in terms of trade on capital markets) is common to most research programs in the neoclassical tradition. That is, the same empirical model applies to all firms. Therefore, tests could not ascertain whether the observed sensitivity of investment to financial variables differs across firms and whether these differences in sensitivity explain the apparently weak relationship between measured user cost and investment. Contemporary empirical studies of information and incentive problems in the investment process have moved beyond the assumption of representative firms by examining firm-level panel data in which firms can be grouped into categories of high and low net worth. For the latter category, changes in net worth or internal funds often appear to affect investment, with underlying investment opportunities (desired investment) held constant.[18] Following Fazzari, Hubbard, and Petersen (1988), empirical researchers have placed firms into groups as a priori financially constrained or financially unconstrained.

Two aspects of this research program's findings are notable regarding measuring incentives to invest. First, numerous empirical studies have found that proxies for internal funds have explanatory power for investment, holding constant Q, the user cost, or accelerator variables (see the review of studies in Hubbard 1998). This suggests that tax policy may have effects on investment by constrained firms beyond those predicted by neoclassical approaches. (Indeed, returning to the accelerator analogy, Bernanke, Gertler, and Gilchrist 1996 argues that this literature describes a "financial accelerator.") In particular, the quantity of internal funds available for investment is supported by the average tax on earnings from existing projects. In this sense, the average as well as the marginal tax rates faced by a firm affect its investment decisions.

Second, empirical studies of financing constraints generally find that the frictionless neoclassical model is rejected only for the groups of firms that a priori are financially constrained (see, for example, Calomiris and Hubbard 1995 and Hubbard, Kashyap, and Whited

1995). In most of the literature, this set of firms accounts for only a small fraction of aggregate investment. While the shadow value of internal funds may not be well captured for some firms in standard representations of the neoclassical approach, the neoclassical model with convex adjustment costs yields reasonable estimated values of marginal adjustment costs for most firms.

Recent developments in this literature have somewhat obscured this conclusion. First, a few authors have presented evidence that appears to expand greatly the set of firms affected by constraints. Gilchrist and Himmelberg (1998), for example, argue that constraints affect a significant share of total investment. Alternatively, Kaplan and Zingales (1997) have argued that the tests for liquidity constraints presented in the literature reveal nothing about liquidity constraints. Indeed, they claim that firms that are extremely healthy by any standard are exactly the firms that look the most constrained in the traditional tests, and that firms of questionable health often look relatively unconstrained.

Further discussion of the tests used puts these efforts into the proper perspective. In a given year some firms experience good news, and some experience bad news. According to efficient market theory, the firms experiencing good news should have all that news reflected in their stock market value and hence in their value of Q. An econometrician could look at a set of firms and pick out those that just experienced good news: their stock market values just increased. The investment models described here would all predict that investment would increase in response to this good news as firms race to increase capacity to meet the surging demand for their product. If the model is true, we can say how much investment should increase in response to the shock to Q, given a prior belief about adjustment costs. If investment increases much less than we expect for

firms without a healthy stock of cash, we might rightly
conclude that these firms do not have ready access to
capital. The trick is constructing the prior belief concerning the "appropriate" investment response; the
sample splitting introduced by Fazzari, Hubbard, and
Petersen (1988) was an ingenious solution to this difficult problem. To establish a reasonable response to a
cash shock, they use the firms unlikely to be constrained,
and then they test whether firms outside that group
seem more responsive to cash.

While the literature regarding financing constraints has gone far, these latest contributions high-
light two important lessons. First, the estimate of the
appropriate investment response is only as good as one's
estimate of Q. Measures of liquidity are important determinants of Q; finding that they are important determinants of investment is compelling only to the extent
that one is convinced that the true Q is also being in-
cluded. As the measure of fundamentals has been re-
fined, these fundamentals have been shown to be more
important determinants of investment. Until recently,
much of the literature about financing constraint used
the measures of Q that produce tiny coefficients, so that
the significance of cash is not conclusive evidence of
liquidity constraints if the refinements presented here
are to be believed.

The Gilchrist and Himmelberg work likely suffers
from mismeasurement of Q; unsurprisingly, they find a
significant cash flow for most firms. Gilchrist and
Himmelberg construct an estimate of marginal Q from
a vector autoregressive regression relating past to future variables. While doing this, they impose the constraint that the past is equally informative about the
present for all firms in their estimation. This condition
is the equivalent of saying that a sales shock to GM (a
highly cyclical firm) affects firm valuation *exactly* the
same as a shock for a small computer start-up firm.

This strong assumption may explain why liquidity variables are especially strong in their study, as they provide an additional peek at true firm fundamentals. The second lesson is that liquidity constraints should not be expected to be most important for financially distressed firms; rather, they should be apparent, should they exist, in firms that want to grow their capital stock faster than the credit markets want to allow. Thus, the Kaplan and Zingales evidence is not the last chapter of the literature, since the cash literature has never suggested that distress and constraints coincide.

In a recent paper that attempted to take these observations into account, Cummins, Hassett, and Oliner (1998) use the forecasts by stock market analysts of future profits to retool Tobin's Q and find that much fluctuation in aggregate investment over time is accounted for by firms that likely do not face liquidity constraints, a conclusion more in line with the original story of Fazzari and colleagues. The exact share of such firms is, however, the subject of continuing debate.

Three recent contributions suggest that liquidity constraint will ultimately be important in models of aggregate investment. Holtz-Eakin, Joulfaian, and Rosen (1994) provide convincing evidence that inheritances increase entrepreneurial activity, a correlation that would not exist if capital markets were perfect, regardless of Q measurement issues. Because small-business entry and exit may well be an important engine for long-run growth, this channel should not be ignored. Hubbard and Gentry (1998) document that the portfolios of entrepreneurs, even wealthy ones, are undiversified and that the portfolio behavior of entrepreneurs is best explained by the existence of costly external finance. Finally, Auerbach and Hassett (1999) provide evidence that firms without bond ratings obey the new view in that their marginal source of finance appears to be retained earnings. Firms with bond ratings appear to obey the old view and to use new share issues and debt as their marginal source of finance. Since firms without bond ratings appear reluctant to employ external finance, an investment behavior identical to that of firms with bond ratings would be surprising.

But the literature regarding constraints has not made a decisive case that constraints are important for the large firms that do the majority of investing. Since constraints are not highly plausible for these companies ex ante, analysis of corporate tax reform will likely provide a reasonable first approximation of any tax effects if the marginal responses identified in the previous section are relied on, at least until the literature concerning financial constraints has reached more of a consensus on these important issues.

Price Elasticity of Capital Goods

One scenario finds that investment incentives might have a small economic impact but at high revenue costs when the increase in investment demand following a tax decrease is offset by a runup in the prices of investment goods. This scenario would be important if the supply of capital goods were fixed or highly inelastic. Much empirical work surveyed above assumed that purchasers of U.S capital goods are price takers. While a perfectly elastic supply function for most individual manufacturers of capital goods is implausible, the effective supply of capital goods to a given domestic market might well be highly elastic in the long run if the world market for capital goods is open.

Goolsbee (1998a) was the first to address this important issue directly. He used disaggregated price and tax data to investigate the extent to which stimulative tax policy is dissipated into the prices of capital goods. Goolsbee finds a significant response of capital goods prices to investment subsidies and concludes that investment tax credits mostly benefit the manufacturers of capital goods.

Using data for the United States and ten other countries, Hassett and Hubbard (1998) find that local investment tax credits have a negligible effect on the prices paid for capital goods; indeed, they find that the prices for capital goods for most countries are highly correlated and that the movements of these over time are consistent with the law of one price. In addition, using disaggregated data on asset-specific prices for capital goods and tax variables for the United States, they find that tax parameters have no effect on the prices for capital goods. The conclusion that U.S. tax policy does not affect the world price of capital goods is especially meaningful, given the relative size of the U.S. economy. Taken together, these tests suggest that the effects of investment tax policy have not been muted in a significant way by upward-sloping supply schedules for capital goods.

Hassett and Hubbard (1998) explore the reasons for their disagreement with Goolsbee. They argue that Goolsbee's price regressions may suffer from spurious regression problems, since the price series used are highly nonstationary and are not cointegrated with the tax variables. When the data are differenced to correct for these factors, Goolsbee's strong relationships disappear. Problems of measurement error, however, are exacerbated by differencing, and debate over the lack of a U.S. price effect continues.

Bondholders

Hines (1998) begins by reinterpreting the empirical evidence summarized in the previous section. According to Hines, Cummins and his colleagues (1994) identify their high elasticities from substitution between tax-favored and tax-disadvantaged assets, as Hines concedes is evident in the data. Suppose that this substitution does take place but that, as evident in figure 2–1, time-series changes in the user cost do not lead to significant swings in investment. How could both observations be true?

Hines argues that traditional models of user cost ignore problems of asymmetric information and bankruptcy. This omission is crucial, because bondholders and equity holders have divergent interests. Equity holders want to maximize after-tax returns, but bondholders want a firm to maximize before-tax returns, since this maximizes the value of the firm if it is in default. Bondholders recognize that an investment tax credit spurs investments that, all else equal, reduce the pretax profitability of the firm and thus reduce payoffs to bondholders if bankruptcy ensues. Anticipating this, bondholders demand that a firm pay them higher interest rates to offset the higher risk. In the Hines model this interest rate response can be large enough that aggregate investment does not respond to an ITC, even though firms move substantially between tax-favored and tax-disadvantaged assets. Hines shows that bond yields responded in the way predicted by his model to the Tax Reform Act of 1986. Since the act removed an equipment subsidy, bondholders in his models should have been pleased. Indeed, at the announcement of the act, interest rates on corporate bonds dropped by fifteen to forty basis points, with lower-grade bond rates dropping more.

Recall that Cummins and his colleagues argue that simultaneity problems make the identification of user-cost elasticity impossible with time-series data alone. They argue that the large elasticities in their studies are consistent with large aggregate elasticities as well and that the concurrent swings in investment and the user cost are not evident in the time-series data because of simultaneity. The Hines model offers a compelling explanation for one channel of such simultaneity, but there are many other potential ones (for example, accelerator effects). Until all plausible effects are identified, precisely predicting the aggregate effects of tax reforms will be difficult.

Too Much Capital

While it is instructive to ask how effective investment incentives are at increasing the fixed capital stock, a more important question remains: What is the social value of the increase in the fixed capital stock? Theoretical research has demonstrated that perfectly competitive economies do not necessarily converge to the correct capital stock. Indeed, Diamond (1965) demonstrates that a competitive economy can reach a steady state with too much capital in the sense that the economy is investing more than it is earning in profit. In this case, individuals can be made better off if they are forced to consume a portion of the capital stock. When evaluating investment incentives, policy analysis must evaluate whether the economy is operating with too much or too little capital.

The classic literature on the golden rule offers benchmarks for guidance. In the approach of Phelps (1961), the golden-rule level of the capital stock relative to output maximizes the level of sustainable per capita consumption. The related Ramsey golden-rule levels of capital maximize the present discounted value of the utility of per capita consumption, and can be less than the Phelps golden-rule levels.

Cohen, Hassett, and Kennedy (1995) compare these golden-rule and actual levels of the capital stock or net investment relative to output to their actual values from 1980 to 1994. Table 4–1, which is excerpted from several tables in that study, indicates that for benchmark

TABLE 4–1
BENCHMARK GOLDEN-RULE AND ACTUAL LEVELS
OF I/Y AND K/Y

Type of Capital	Golden-Rule Level		Actual Level (1980–1994 average)
	Phelps	Ramsey	
Net Investment as Percentage of GDP			
Total fixed	8.3	6.0	4.2
Business fixed	4.8	3.6	2.4
Producers' durable equipment	2.4	2.0	1.3
Nonresidential structures	2.0	1.3	1.2
Residential	2.7	1.6	1.8
Ratio of Capital Stock to GDP			
Total fixed	3.3	2.4	1.9
Business fixed	1.9	1.4	1.0
Producers' durable equipment	1.0	0.8	0.5
Nonresidential structures	0.8	0.5	0.5
Residential	1.1	0.6	0.9

NOTE: Benchmark parameter values are labor force growth rate = 0.01; rate of labor-augmenting technical change = 0.15; social dis-. count rate = 0.12; and social intertemporal elasticity of substitution (Φ) = 3. Further, $\alpha_{\text{total fixed}} = 0.30$; $\alpha_{\text{business fixed}} = 0.24$; $\alpha_{\text{equipment}} = 0.18$; $\alpha_{\text{structures}} = 0.06$; and $\alpha_{\text{residential}} = 0.06$.
Source: Cohen, Hassett, and Kennedy 1995, table 2.

parameter values, equipment investment and capital stocks are below their golden-rule levels (assuming 1980–1994 is sufficiently long to characterize a steady state), while residential investment and the residential capital stocks—which have received significant tax subsidies over this period—are near or above their golden-rule levels. Cohen, Hassett, and Kennedy also show that these conclusions are not changed if the key parameters are allowed to vary across a broad range of plausible values.

Alternatively, several authors have attempted to evaluate the optimality of the U.S. capital stock by relating various interest rates to the growth rate of the gross domestic product in the steady state. According to the golden rule, these should equal one another. If there is too much capital, the interest rate will be lower than the growth rate; if there is too little, the interest rate is greater than the growth rate. On the one hand, Tobin (1965), Solow (1970), and Feldstein (1977) argue that the marginal productivity of capital obtained from estimates of accounting profits is about 10 percent, well above the interest rate and at a level that suggests too little capital. On the other hand, Ibbotson (1987) calculates a mean return on U.S. Treasury bills from 1926 to 1986 of only 0.3 percent, which suggests too much capital. The answer to the question of whether to use interest rates and stock market returns depends critically on the relevant weights associated to each return and on the impact of risk, and those difficulties suggest that this approach may not lead to decisive conclusions.

Abel, Mankiw, Summers, and Zeckhauser (1989) pursue an alternative strategy for evaluating whether the U.S. capital stock is greater or less than the optimal level. In a stochastic setting with a general production technology, they demonstrate that an economy is dynamically inefficient if it invests more than the returns from capital. They show that the economy is dynamically efficient—and hence in the range in which stimulative tax policy might have positive social returns—if the returns from capital exceed investment. With their terminology, the key question is whether the capital stock is on balance a sink or a spout. This observation is useful, because it allows for judgment about dynamic efficiency based on readily observable cash flows. Abel

and his colleagues conclude that the economy is dynamically efficient. Thus, data for both capital stock and cash
flow suggest that by raising the stock of equipment capital, investment incentives may have positive social
returns.[19]

5

Policy Implications

The finding of significant short-term and long-term effects of the user cost of capital on equipment investment suggests applications to current policy debates. In this section, I evaluate consequences for the user cost and for the investment of a reduction in inflation and a switch from an income tax to a broad-based consumption tax.

Low Inflation as an Investment Subsidy

Many economists (see, for example, Feldstein 1976 and King and Fullerton 1984) have argued that, under fairly general assumptions, a reduction in the rate of inflation provides a relatively costless stimulus to business fixed investment by reducing the user cost of capital. Expected inflation affects investment decisions through three channels. First, user cost increases with inflation, because depreciation allowances are fixed nominally and future deductions are worth less when inflation increases. Second, inflation increases the cost of equity finance, since nominal capital gains are taxed. Third, inflation affects the real cost of borrowing to purchase machines.

Calculating the negative effects of higher inflation

on the present value of depreciation deductions is a simple present-value exercise, with interest rates held constant. The impact of inflation on the cost of equity finance is similarly straightforward. The total effect of inflation on investment, however, is quite difficult to pin down. The effect of inflation on user cost cannot be precisely calculated without knowing the effect on the interest rate, and this channel is still poorly understood.

The literature has produced two theories that purport to explain how interest rates respond to changes in inflation. The first, the Fisher effect, states that the interest rate rises one for one with the inflation rate. In this view, the real interest rate does not depend on inflation. The second possibility is that an after-tax Fisher effect holds. In this view, because the real after-tax interest rate is independent of inflation, the nominal interest rate increases by more than the rate of inflation when inflation changes.

If the Fisher effect holds, then higher inflation reduces the after-tax cost of borrowing for firms, and the total effect of inflation on user cost is of uncertain direction. The reduction occurs because interest payments are deductible for firms and the higher nominal interest rate translates into a bigger tax deduction, with the real before-tax interest rate held constant. If the after-tax Fisher effect holds, then firms receive an extra tax benefit as inflation increases, and the harmful effects of higher inflation through the other channels dominate the movements of user cost. Tests performed to date have been able to reject the hypothesis that inflation has no effect on user cost, but they have not been able to provide conclusive evidence for either of the two explanatory Fisher effects.[20]

Cohen, Hassett, and Hubbard (1998) calculate the marginal effects on the user cost of lowering inflation and explore the effects of differing assumptions on their conclusions.[21] They estimate that the current value of user cost for equipment investment is about 0.22, and they conclude that a permanent decrease in inflation of one percentage point lowers user cost by about one-half percentage point, assuming that the after-tax Fisher effect holds. In their calculations, the incremental effect of each additional reduction in inflation of one percentage point is approximately the same. Thus, if the annual inflation rate were reduced from 4 percent to 0, user cost of capital would decline about two percentage points—proportionally by about 10 percent. Given the elasticity estimates reviewed in the previous section, this tax cut would provide a significant stimulus to investment. Conversely, if the pure Fisher effect holds, then the stimulus of lower inflation would be small.

Moving to a Consumption Tax

Under the current U.S. income tax system, the user cost of capital is influenced by the corporate tax rate, investment tax credits, and the present value of depreciation allowances. Under a broad-based consumption tax, firms pay tax on the difference between receipts and purchases from other firms. That is, there is no investment tax credit, and investment is expensed. In this case (assuming that the corporate tax rate does not change over time), the user cost of capital no longer depends on taxes. That is, under a consumption tax, taxes do not distort business investment decisions; investment decisions are based solely on nontax fundamentals. Since U.S. tax policy currently increases user cost, the switch to the consumption tax lowers user cost and increases investment.

By how much? Under current law and assuming that the output price and the capital-goods price are both equal to unity, then for assets with seven-year lives (assuming that the expected real interest rate is 4 percent, the expected inflation rate is 3 percent, and the marginal machine is financed half with equity and half with debt) the value of the tax wedge under 1996 U.S. tax law is 1.148, and the user cost of capital is 0.234. The move to the consumption tax would lower the value of user cost to 0.205, a reduction that would lead, *ceteris paribus*, to about a 10 percent increase in equipment investment, given the consensus estimates.

Other aggregate variables are likely to change in response to such a major alteration to the tax code. Nominal interest rates and the supply of savings, for example, would likely change. While estimating the net stimulus to investment is difficult, the consensus of the recent literature concerning investment suggests that the partial equilibrium impact on investment may be quite large.

Temporary Tax Incentives?

The discussion thus far pertains to permanent changes in investment incentives. Even a casual observation of the history of investment incentives since the 1950s suggests the usefulness of considering temporary investment incentives. Since 1962, the mean duration of a typical state with an ITC in effect has been about three and one-half years, and the mean duration of the no-ITC state has been about the same length. Most recently, President George Bush in 1992 advocated a modified ITC, known as the investment tax allowance, and President William Clinton in early 1993 proposed an incremental ITC; neither measure was enacted.

What is the likely impact on aggregate capital accumulation of temporary investment incentives? Temporary investment incentives can have even larger short-run impacts on investment than permanent investment incentives (see Auerbach 1989a). Consider a temporary ITC known to last one period. The ITC lowers the current user cost both through its effect on the price of purchasing a machine today and through the consequences of its removal tomorrow. Firms will race to buy before the credit is removed.

The great potential effects of temporary tax incentives on investment do not imply that they are desirable tax policy—even if one believes that long-run investment incentives are sound tax policy. In the presence of uncertainty and adjustment costs, there is little reason to believe that policymakers can time investment incentives for the purposes of a stabilization policy. Moreover, the use of temporary incentives increases uncertainty in business capital budgeting and makes it more difficult for firms to forecast the path of the user cost of capital.

What if firms do not know the exact timing of changes in investment incentives; that is, if tax policy is uncertain? A substantial literature evaluates the effects of price uncertainty on investment; the lesson from this literature is that the sign of the effect of uncertainty on investment depends crucially on assumptions about adjustment costs and returns to scale. Hartman (1972) shows that uncertainty generally increases investment in a model with constant returns and convex adjustment costs. Abel (1983) derives a similar result in continuous time. Pindyck (1988), however, shows that uncertainty can significantly lower capital formation if investment is irreversible and if returns to scale are decreasing. I described Pindyck's intuition earlier: in an uncertain world there is a gain to delaying investment—the option value of waiting—and the higher the variance in the output price, the higher is this gain.

Thus, one might be tempted to conclude from the early contributions to this literature that the predicted effect of tax policy uncertainty depends on what is believed about the reversibility of capital investments. Strictly speaking, however, tax policy about uncertainty can even increase investment in the models of Hartman, Abel, and Pindyck (see Hassett and Metcalf 1994, 1999).

This difference arises because uncertainty about tax policy differs from uncertainty about price in an important way. Researchers often introduce uncertainty by assuming that price follows a continuous-time random walk (Brownian motion or geometric Brownian motion). When price follows a random walk, the appropriate forecast of rational expectations for price at any time in the future is today's price, and the future path of price is unbounded. Unlike most prices, tax parameters tend to remain constant for a few years and then jump to new values. In addition, jumps in the ITC tend to be mean-reverting: when credit is high, it is likely to be reduced in the future; when credit is low, it is likely to be increased in the future. Because of these properties, the normal gain to waiting in a model with irreversibility is reduced significantly with an investment tax credit: since a firm fears that the credit might be eliminated, it is more likely to invest today while the credit is still effective. Hassett and Metcalf demonstrate that this effect dominates the reverse effect in the state without investment tax credit and conclude that increasing the uncertainty of tax policy raises aggregate investment.

As with temporary investment incentives generally, this result does not imply that a random tax policy is desirable. Most existing studies analyze investment in a partial equilibrium setting without utility costs to bunching capital formation. Bizer and Judd (1989) show that, in a general equilibrium setting, a random investment tax policy significantly reduces welfare. The randomness has a negative impact, because consumers wish to smooth consumption, and fluctuations in investment credits make smoothing costly.

6
Conclusions

The study of business investment has advanced significantly in a short time. Ten years ago, almost no economist believed that investment demand elasticity differed much from zero. In a recent survey of specialists in labor and public economics (Fuchs, Krueger, and Poterba 1997), the median respondent indicated that a decline in user cost from a switch to expensing would increase investment by an amount consistent with an elasticity of about one. Perhaps this response reflects the strong biases of economists, but the literature surveyed here certainly has contributed explanations to the survey result. A consensus that investment demand is sensitive to taxation has been reached, and years of work on neoclassical-style models have paid significant dividends. While uncertainty concerning the likely impact on tax reform or labor supply and productivity remains, there is, nonetheless, a strong case to be made that a switch to a flat tax could produce significant effects of positive growth—investment would likely surge.

The exact nature of adjustment costs and the likely short-run effects of tax reforms have not been identified definitively, but the long-run effects of tax policy on investment demand are, for now at least, fairly clear.

Before we can say with certainty that tax cuts will increase investment, however, we need a much clearer picture of how interest rates, output, and the stock market respond. The work to acquire this knowledge is naturally of a high degree of difficulty.

Notes

1. In most formulations the expression $\rho\delta$ is omitted, because it is assumed to be small and also because it vanishes in continuous time.

2. Third, a higher corporate tax rate increases the value of interest deductions and hence, all else being equal, reduces the real cost of debt finance, ρ_d. Given realistic parameter values, however, the first effect dominates: on balance, corporate taxes increase the user cost or the minimum pretax marginal product of capital necessary to yield an acceptable real rate of return to investors. As a consequence, corporate taxes in the United States diminish the incentive to invest.

3. To be more specific, Jorgenson assumed that the revenue function of the firm was Cobb-Douglas and that the firm set marginal revenue (regarding capital) equal to user cost to maximize profits.

4. Haavelmo (1960), for example, writes: "The demand for investment cannot simply be derived from the demand for capital ... I think the sooner this naive and unfounded theory of the demand for investment schedule is abandoned, the sooner we shall have a chance of making some real progress in constructing more powerful theories to deal with the capricious short-run variations in the rate of private investment" (quoted in Jorgenson 1967, 133).

5. See, for example, Bosworth 1985; Bernanke, Bohn, and Reiss 1988; and the survey in Chirinko 1993. The often poor empirical performance of Q models has led some researchers to abandon the assumptions of reversible investment and convex costs used in testing neoclassical models in favor of approaches based on lumpy and "irreversible" investment. See, for example, the discussions and reviews of studies in Pindyck 1991, Dixit and Pindyck 1994, and Hubbard 1994.

6. In an alternative representation, Feldstein (1982) explored the effects of effective tax rates on investment in reduced-form models; for a critique of this approach, see Chirinko 1987.

7. Eisner and Strotz (1963) offer an early discussion of adjustment costs. The theory was developed and extended by Lucas (1967, 1976), Gould (1968), Treadway (1969, 1970), Uzawa (1969), Mortenson (1973), Abel (1980), and Hayashi (1982). Researchers have generally assumed convex costs of adjusting the capital stock; the idea is that it is more costly to implement a given increment to the capital stock quickly rather than gradually. I discuss alternative assumptions about adjustment costs in chapter 4.

8. As noted, Hayashi (1982) provided the conditions required to equate marginal Q with average Q, which is observable because it depends on the market valuation of the firm's assets. Summers (1981) incorporated additional tax parameters in the Q model.

9. The measure of Q plotted here is constructed from data from the Federal Reserve's flow of funds accounts.

10. If the growth rate of business fixed investment is regressed on many lags of the growth rate of Q, the sum of the coefficients is about 0.1, implying that a 20 percent increase in the growth rate of Q would lead to a prediction of about a 2 percent higher growth rate of business fixed investment. Cochrane (1991) finds significantly larger effects of the growth of Q on the growth of total private investment. The results differ because Cochrane's measure of investment includes residential investment, which is—perhaps surprisingly—more highly correlated with stock market fluctuations.

11. Cummins, Hassett, and Hubbard (1994, 1995) also use this approach in a user-cost model. For U.S. data, they estimate a user-cost coefficient of about −0.65.

12. This is a test of the restricted model against the alternative model that current profits have explanatory power for investment beyond their ability to predict future profits. Gilchrist and Himmelberg find that cash flow is an independent fundamental and that excess sensitivity of investment to cash flow is a characteristic of firms that they identify as constrained—measured by size, bond rating, commercial paper rating, or dividend payout.

13. The seeds of this literature are much older. Rothschild (1971), for example, writes: "Convex cost-of-adjustment functions may help to explain why Rome was not built in a day. However, there is no clear saving and may be some loss to spreading the work of installing a button on a shirt over several weeks." His "bang-bang" model of investment provides an early example of a "lumpy investment" model.

14. In earlier work Doms and Dunne (1994) report that plant-level investment data exhibit skewness and kurtosis consistent with investment being somewhat lumpy.

15. To calculate the desired capital stock for each firm, Caballero, Engel, and Haltiwanger use plant-level output data and two-digit Jorgensonian user costs constructed from the tax data used in Cummins, Hassett, and Hubbard 1994 and Goolsbee 1998a.

16. Because their mandated investment measure is the same as that in a frictionless neoclassical model, their tests—while sugges-

tive—neither confirm nor reject the presence of convex adjustment costs. First, mandated investment itself depends on adjustment costs. Second, if adjustment costs were present, mandated investment also depends on future values of tax parameters

17. Goolsbee (1998a) provides support for this view, but Hassett and Hubbard (1998) provide contradictory evidence. I return to this debate below.

18. For reviews of the theoretical literature, see Bernanke, Gertler, and Gilchrist 1996 and Hubbard 1990, 1994.

19. Because the golden-rule models are developed for a closed economy, it is difficult to extend the comparison to domestic and foreign fixed capital.

20. Cohen, Hassett, and Hubbard (1998) discuss the existing evidence and present tests of the two Fisher effects.

21. Earlier empirical studies of the effect of inflation on real business tax burdens include Feldstein and Summers 1979 and Auerbach 1983b. Cohen, Hassett, and Hubbard (1998) also allow for inflation to increase taxes paid because of the effects of inflation on the cost of carrying inventories.

References

Abel, Andrew B. 1980. "Empirical Investment Equations: An Integrative Framework." *Journal of Monetary Economics* 12 (spring): 39–91.

———. 1983. "Optimal Investment under Uncertainty." *American Economic Review* 73 (March): 228–33.

———. 1990. "Consumption and Investment." In *Handbook of Monetary Economics*, edited by Benjamin M. Friedman and Frank H. Hahn. Vol. 2. Amsterdam: North-Holland.

Abel, Andrew B., and Olivier J. Blanchard. 1986. "The Present Value of Profits and Cyclical Movements in Investment." *Econometrica* 54 (March): 249–73.

Abel, Andrew B., and Janice C. Eberly. 1995. "Optimal Investment with Costly Irreversibility." Working Paper 5091, National Bureau of Economic Research.

———. 1996. "Investment and q with Fixed Costs: An Empirical Analysis." Philadelphia: Wharton School. Mimeographed.

Abel, Andrew B., N. Gregory Mankiw, Lawrence H. Summers, and Richard J. Zeckhauser. 1989. "Assessing Dynamic Efficiency: Theory and Evidence." *Review of Economic Studies* 56: 1–20.

Aftalian, A. 1909. "La réalité des surproductions générales, essai d'une théorie des crises générales et périodiques." *Revue d'Economie Politique.*

Auerbach, Alan J. 1983a. "Corporate Taxation in the United States." *Brookings Papers on Economic Activity* 2: 451–513.

———. 1983b. "Taxation, Corporate Financial Policy, and the Cost of Capital." *Journal of Economic Literature* 21 (September): 905–40.

———. 1989a. "Tax Reform and Adjustment Costs: The Impact on Investment and Market Value." *International Economic Review* 30: 939–62.

———. 1989b. "The Deadweight Loss from 'Non-Neutral' Capital Income Taxation." *Journal of Public Economics* 40: 1–36.

Auerbach, Alan J., and Kevin A. Hassett. 1991. "Recent U.S. Investment Behavior and the Tax Reform Act of 1986: A Disaggregate View." *Carnegie-Rochester Conference Series on Public Policy* 35 (autumn): 185–215.

———. 1999. "On the Marginal Source of Investment Funds." Mimeographed.

Barnett, Steven A., and Plutarchos Sakellaris. 1995. "Nonlinear Response of Firm Investment to *Q*: Testing a Model of Convex and Nonconvex Adjustment Costs." Working Paper 95-11, University of Maryland.

Bernanke, Ben, Henning Bohn, and Peter C. Reiss. 1988. "Alternative Nonnested Specification Tests of Time-Series Investment Models." *Journal of Econometrics* 37 (March): 293–326.

Bernanke, Ben, Mark Gertler, and Simon Gilchrist. 1996. "The Financial Accelerator and the Flight to Quality." *Review of Economics and Statistics* 78 (1) (February): 1–15.

Bertola, Giuseppe, and Ricardo Caballero. 1990. "Kinked Adjustment Costs and Aggregate Dynamics." *NBER Macroeconomics Annual,* pp. 237–88.

Bizer, David, and Kenneth Judd. 1989. "Taxation and Uncertainty." *American Economic Review* 79 (May): 331–36.

Bond, Stephen, and Costas Meghir. 1994. "Dynamic Investment Models and the Firm's Financial Policy." *Review of Economic Studies* 61: 197–222.

Bosworth, Barry P. 1985. "Taxes and the Investment Recovery." *Brookings Papers on Economic Activity* 1: 1–38.

Caballero, Ricardo J. 1994. "Small Sample Bias and Adjustment Costs." *Review of Economics and Statistics* 76 (1) (February): 52–58.

Caballero, Ricardo J., Eduardo M. R. A. Engel, and John C. Haltiwanger. 1995. "Plant-Level Adjustment and Aggregate Investment Dynamics." *Brookings Papers on Economic Activity* 2: 1–54.

Calomiris, Charles W., and R. Glenn Hubbard. 1995. "Internal Finance and Investment: Evidence from the Undistributed Profits Tax of 1937–1938." *Journal of Business* 68 (October): 443–82.

Chirinko, Robert S. 1987. "The Ineffectiveness of Effective Tax Rates on Business Investment: A Critique of Feldstein's Fisher-Schultz Lecture." *Journal of Public Economics* 32: 369–87.

———. 1993. "Business Fixed Investment Spending: Modeling Strategies, Empirical Results, and Policy Implications." *Journal of Economic Literature* 31 (December): 1875–911.

Chirinko, Robert S., and Robert Eisner. 1983. "Tax Policy in Major Macroeconomic Models." *Journal of Public Economics* 20: 139–66.

Clark, J. M. 1917. "Business Acceleration and the Law of Demand." *Journal of Political Economy* 25 (March): 217–35.

Clark, Peter K. 1993. "Tax Incentives and Equipment Investment." *Brookings Papers on Economic Activity* 1: 317–39.

Cochrane, John. 1991. "Production-Based Asset Pricing and the Link between Stock Returns and Economic Fluctuations." *Journal of Finance* 46 (March): 209–37.

Cohen, Darrel, Kevin A. Hassett, and R. Glenn Hubbard. 1998. "Inflation and the User Cost of Capital: Does Inflation Still Matter?" Columbia University. Mimeographed.

Cohen, Darrel, Kevin A. Hassett, and James Kennedy. 1995. "Are U.S. Investment and Capital Stocks at Their Optimal Levels?" FEDS Working Paper 9532, Board of Governors of the Federal Reserve System.

Cummins, Jason G., and Mathew Dey. 1998. "Taxation, Investment, and Firm Growth with Heterogeneous Capital." New York University. Mimeographed.

Cummins, Jason G., Trevor S. Harris, and Kevin A. Hassett. 1995. "Accounting Standards, Information Flow, and Firm Investment Behavior." In *The Effects of Taxation on Multinational Corporations*, edited by Martin Feldstein, James R. Hines, and R. Glenn Hubbard. Chicago: University of Chicago Press.

Cummins, Jason G., Kevin A. Hassett, and R. Glenn Hubbard. 1994. "A Reconsideration of Investment Behavior Using Tax Reforms as Natural Experiments." *Brookings Papers on Economic Activity* 2: 1–74.

———. 1995. "Have Tax Reforms Affected Investment?" In *Tax Policy and the Economy*, edited by James M. Poterba. Vol. 9. Cambridge: MIT Press.

———. 1996. "Tax Reforms and Investment: A Cross-Country Comparison." *Journal of Public Economics* 62: 237–73.

Cummins, Jason G., Kevin A. Hassett, and Stephen Oliner. 1998. "Investment Behavior, Internal Funds, and Observable Expectations." New York University. Mimeographed.

Cummins, Jason G., and R. Glenn Hubbard. 1995. "The Tax Sensitivity of Foreign Direct Investment: Evidence from Firm-Level Panel Data." In *The Effects of Taxation on Multinational Corporations,* edited by Martin Feldstein, James R. Hines, and R. Glenn Hubbard. Chicago: University of Chicago Press.

Diamond, Peter A. 1965. "National Debt in a Neoclassical Growth Model." *American Economic Review* 55 (December): 1126–50.

Dixit, Avinash K., and Robert S. Pindyck. 1994. *Investment under Uncertainty.* Princeton: Princeton University Press.

Doms, Mark, and Timothy Dunne. 1994. "Capital Adjustment Patterns in Manufacturing Plants." Discussion Paper 94-11, U.S. Bureau of the Census, Center for Economic Studies.

Doyle, Joanne, and Toni M. Whited. 1998. "Fixed Costs of Adjustment, Coordination, and Industry Investment." James Madison University. Mimeographed.

Eisner, Robert. 1969. "Tax Policy and Investment Behavior: Comment." *American Economic Review* 59 (June): 379–88.

———. 1970. "Tax Policy and Investment Behavior: Further Comment." *American Economic Review* 60 (September): 746–52.

Eisner, Robert, and M. Ishaq Nadiri. 1968. "Investment Behavior and Neoclassical Theory." *Review of Economics and Statistics* 50: 369–82.

———. 1970. "Neoclassical Theory of Investment Behavior: A Comment." *Review of Economics and Statistics* 52 (May): 216–22.

Eisner, Robert, and Robert H. Strotz. 1963. "Determinants of Business Investment." In *Impacts of Monetary Policy,* prepared for the Commission on Money and Credit. Englewood Cliffs, N.J.: Prentice-Hall.

Fallick, Bruce C., and Kevin A. Hassett. Forthcoming. "Is Unionization a Tax on Profits? Investment Responses to Union Certification." *Journal of Labor Economics.*

Fazzari, Steven M., R. Glenn Hubbard, and Bruce C. Petersen. 1988. "Financing Constraints and Corporate Investment." *Brookings Papers on Economic Activity* 1: 141–95.

Feldstein, Martin S. 1976. "Inflation, Income Taxes, and the Rate of Interest: A Theoretical Analysis." *American Economic Review* 66 (June): 8809–20.

———. 1977. "Does the United States Save Too Little?" *American Economic Review* 67 (May): 116–21.

———. 1982. "Inflation, Tax Rules, and Investment: Some Econometric Evidence." *Econometrica* 50 (July): 825–62.

Feldstein, Martin S., and Lawrence H. Summers. 1979. "Inflation and the Taxation of Capital Income in the Corporate Sector." *National Tax Journal* 32 (December): 445–70.

Fisher, Irving. 1930. *The Theory of Interest.* New York: Macmillan.

Fuchs, Victor R., Alan B. Krueger, and James M. Poterba. 1997. "Why Do Economists Disagree about Policy? The Roles of Beliefs about Parameters and Values." NBER Working Paper 6151, National Bureau of Economic Research.

Gilchrist, Simon. 1991. "An Empirical Analysis of Corporate Investment and Financing Hierarchies Using Firm-Level Panel Data." Board of Governors of the Federal Reserve System. Mimeographed.

Gilchrist, Simon, and Charles P. Himmelberg. 1995. "Evidence on the Role of Cash Flow in Reduced-Form Investment Equations." *Journal of Monetary Economics* 36: 541–72.

———. 1998. "Investment Fundamentals and Finance."

NBER Working Paper 6652, National Bureau of Economic Research.

Goolsbee, Austan. 1998a. "Investment Tax Incentives and the Price of Capital Goods." *Quarterly Journal of Economics* 113 (1) (February): 121–48.

———. 1998b. "Measurement Error and the Cost of Capital." University of Chicago. Mimeographed.

Goolsbee, Austan, and David B. Gross. 1997. "Estimating Adjustment Costs with Data on Heterogeneous Capital Goods." NBER Working Paper 6342, National Bureau of Economic Research.

Gould, John P. 1968. "Adjustment Costs in the Theory of Investment of the Firm." *Review of Economic Studies* 35: 47–55.

Griliches, Zvi, and Jerry A. Hausman. 1986. "Errors in Variables in Panel Data." *Journal of Econometrics* 31 (February): 141–54.

Haavelmo, Trygve. 1960. *A Study in the Theory of Investment*. Chicago: University of Chicago Press.

Hall, Robert E., and Dale W. Jorgenson. 1967. "Tax Policy and Investment Behavior." *American Economic Review* 57 (June): 391–414.

Hartman, Richard. 1972. "The Effects of Price and Cost Uncertainty on Investment." *Journal of Economic Theory* 5: 258–66.

Hassett, Kevin A., and R. Glenn Hubbard. 1997. "Tax Policy and Investment." In *Fiscal Policy Lessons from Economic Research*, edited by Alan J. Auerbach, pp. 339–86. Cambridge: MIT Press.

———. 1998. "Are Investment Incentives Blunted by Changes in Prices of Capital Goods?" *International Finance* 1 (1) (October): 103–26.

Hassett, Kevin A., and Gilbert E. Metcalf. 1994. "Investment with Uncertain Tax Policy: Does Random Tax Policy Discourage Investment?" Working Paper 4780, National Bureau of Economic Research.

————. 1999. "Investment with Uncertain Tax Policy: Does Random Tax Policy Discourage Investment?" *Economic Journal* 109 (July): 1–22.

Hayashi, Fumio. 1982. "Tobin's Marginal Q and Average Q: A Neoclassical Interpretation." *Econometrica* 50 (January): 213–24.

Hines, James R. 1998. "Investment Ramifications of Distortionary Tax Subsidies." Working Paper 6615, National Bureau of Economic Research.

Holtz-Eakin, Douglas, David Joulfaian, and Harvey Rosen. 1994. "Entrepreneurial Decisions and Liquidity Constraints." Working Paper 4526, National Bureau of Economic Research.

Hubbard, R. Glenn. 1990. "Introduction." In *Asymmetric Information, Corporate Finance, and Investment*, edited by R. Glenn Hubbard. Chicago: University of Chicago Press.

————. 1994. "Investment under Uncertainty: Keeping One's Options Open." *Journal of Economic Literature* 32 (December): 1816–31.

————. 1998. "Capital-Market Imperfections and Investment." *Journal of Economic Literature* 36 (March): 193–225.

Hubbard, R. Glenn, and William M. Gentry. 1998. "Fundamental Tax Reform and Corporate Financial Policy." Working Paper 6433, National Bureau of Economic Research.

Hubbard, R. Glenn, and Anil K. Kashyap. 1992. "Internal Net Worth and the Investment Process: An Application to U.S. Agriculture." *Journal of Political Economy* 100 (June): 506–34.

Hubbard, R. Glenn, Anil K. Kashyap, and Toni M. Whited. 1995. "Internal Finance and Firm Investment." *Journal of Money, Credit, and Banking* 27 (August): 683–701.

Hulten, Charles R., and Frank C. Wykoff. 1981. "The Measurement of Economic Depreciation." In *Depreciation, Inflation, and the Taxation of Income from Capital*, edited by Charles R. Hulten. Washington, D.C.: Urban Institute.

Ibbotson, R. G. 1987. *Stocks, Bonds, Bills, and Inflation: Market Results for 1926–1986*. Chicago: Ibbotson and Associates, Inc.

Jorgenson, Dale W. 1963. "Capital Theory and Investment Behavior." *American Economic Review* 53 (May): 247–59.

————. 1967. "Theory of Investment Behavior." In *Determinants of Investment Behavior*, edited by Robert Ferber. New York: Columbia University Press.

Judd, Kenneth L. 1995. "The Optimal Tax Rate for Capital Income Is Negative." Working paper. Stanford: Hoover Institution.

Kaplan, Steven N., and Luigi Zingales. 1997. "Do Financing Constraints Explain Why Investment Is Correlated with Cash Flow?" *Quarterly Journal of Economics* (February): 169–215.

King, Mervyn A., and Don Fullerton, eds. 1984. *The Taxation of Income from Capital: A Comparative Study of the United States, United Kingdom, Sweden, and West Germany*. Chicago: University of Chicago Press.

Lucas, Robert E., Jr. 1967. "Adjustment Costs and the Theory of Supply." *Journal of Political Economy* 75 (August): 321–34.

————. 1976. "Econometric Policy Evaluation: A Critique." In *The Phillips Curve and Labor Markets*, edited by Karl Brunner and Allan Meltzer. Carnegie-Rochester Conference Series on Public Policy. Vol. 1, pp. 19–46.

Meyer, John R., and Edwin Kuh. 1957. *The Investment Decision*. Cambridge: Harvard University Press.

Modigliani, Franco, and Merton H. Miller. 1958. "The Cost of Capital, Corporation Finance and the Theory of Investment." *American Economic Review* 48 (June): 261–97.

Mortenson, Dale T. 1973. "Generalized Costs of Adjustment and Dynamic Factor Demand Theory." *Econometrica* 41: 657–67.

Phelps, Edmund S. 1961. "The Golden Rule of Accumulation: A Fable for Growth Men." *American Economic Review* 51: 638–43.

Pindyck, Robert S. 1988. "Irreversible Investment, Capacity Choice, and the Value of the Firm." *American Economic Review* 78 (December): 969–85.

———. 1991. "Irreversibility, Uncertainty, and Investment." *Journal of Economic Literature* 29 (September): 1110–48.

Pindyck, Robert S., and Julio J. Rotemberg. 1983. "Dynamic Factor Demands under Rational Expectations." *Scandinavian Journal of Economics* 85: 223–38.

Rothschild, Michael. 1971. "On the Costs of Adjusting the Capital Stock." *Quarterly Journal of Economics* 85: 6056–61.

Salinger, Michael A., and Lawrence H. Summers. 1983. "Tax Reform and Corporate Investment: A Microeconomic Simulation Study." In *Behavioral Simulation Methods in Tax Policy Analysis,* edited by Martin Feldstein. Chicago: University of Chicago Press.

Shapiro, Matthew D. 1986. "The Dynamic Demand for Capital and Labor." *Quarterly Journal of Economics* 101 (August): 513–47.

Solow, Robert. 1970. *Growth Theory*. Oxford: Oxford University Press.

Stock, James H., and Mark W. Watson. 1993. "A Simple
MLE of Cointegrating Vectors in Higher Order
Integrated Systems." *Econometrica* 61 (January):
111–52.

Summers, Lawrence H. 1981. "Taxation and Corporate
Investment: A *Q*-Theory Approach." *Brookings
Papers on Economic Activity* 1: 67–127.

———. 1987. "Investment Incentives and the Discount-
ing of Depreciation Allowances." In *The Effects of
Taxation on Capital Accumulation,* edited by Martin Feldstein. Chicago: University of Chicago Press.

Tobin, James. 1965. "Economic Growth as an Objective of
Government Policy." In *Essays in Economics. Vol. 1:
Macroeconomics.* Amsterdam: North-Holland.

———. 1969. "A General Equilibrium Approach to Monetary Theory." *Journal of Money, Credit, and Banking* 1 (February): 15–29.

Treadway, A. B. 1969. "On Rational Entrepreneurial
Behavior and the Demand for Investment." *Review
of Economic Studies* 36: 227–39.

———. 1970. "Adjustment Cost and Variable Imports
in the Theory of the Competitive Firm." *Journal of
Economic Theory* 2: 329–47.

Uzawa, H. 1969. "Time Preference and the Penrose Effect in a Two-Class Model of Economic Growth."
Journal of Political Economy 77: 628–52.

Whited, Toni M. 1992. "Debt, Liquidity Constraints, and
Corporate Investment." *Journal of Finance* 47 (September): 1425–60.

About the Author

KEVIN A. HASSETT is a resident scholar at the American Enterprise Institute. He had been a senior economist at the Board of Governors of the Federal Reserve System and an associate professor of economics at the Graduate School of Business, Columbia University. He was a policy consultant to the Treasury Department during the Bush and the Clinton administrations.

His work in identifying the effects of government policies on business investment behavior has strongly supported the view that the current structure of corporate taxation significantly reduces capital formation and economic growth.

The author's articles have appeared in professional journals, including the *Quarterly Journal of Economics* and the *Journal of Public Economics,* as well as in popular publications, including *Investor's Business Daily,* the *Wall Street Journal,* and the *Weekly Standard.*

AEI STUDIES ON TAX REFORM
R. Glenn Hubbard and Diana Furchtgott-Roth
Series Editors

ASSESSING THE EFFECTIVENESS OF SAVING INCENTIVES
R. Glenn Hubbard and Jonathan S. Skinner

DISTRIBUTIONAL IMPLICATIONS OF A CONSUMPTION TAX
William M. Gentry and R. Glenn Hubbard

FUNDAMENTAL ISSUES IN CONSUMPTION TAXATION
David F. Bradford

TAXATION OF FINANCIAL SERVICES UNDER A
CONSUMPTION TAX
Peter R. Merrill

TAXING CONSUMPTION IN A GLOBAL ECONOMY
Harry Grubert and T. Scott Newlon

TAX POLICY AND INVESTMENT
Kevin A. Hassett